I0824236

Kwanzaa

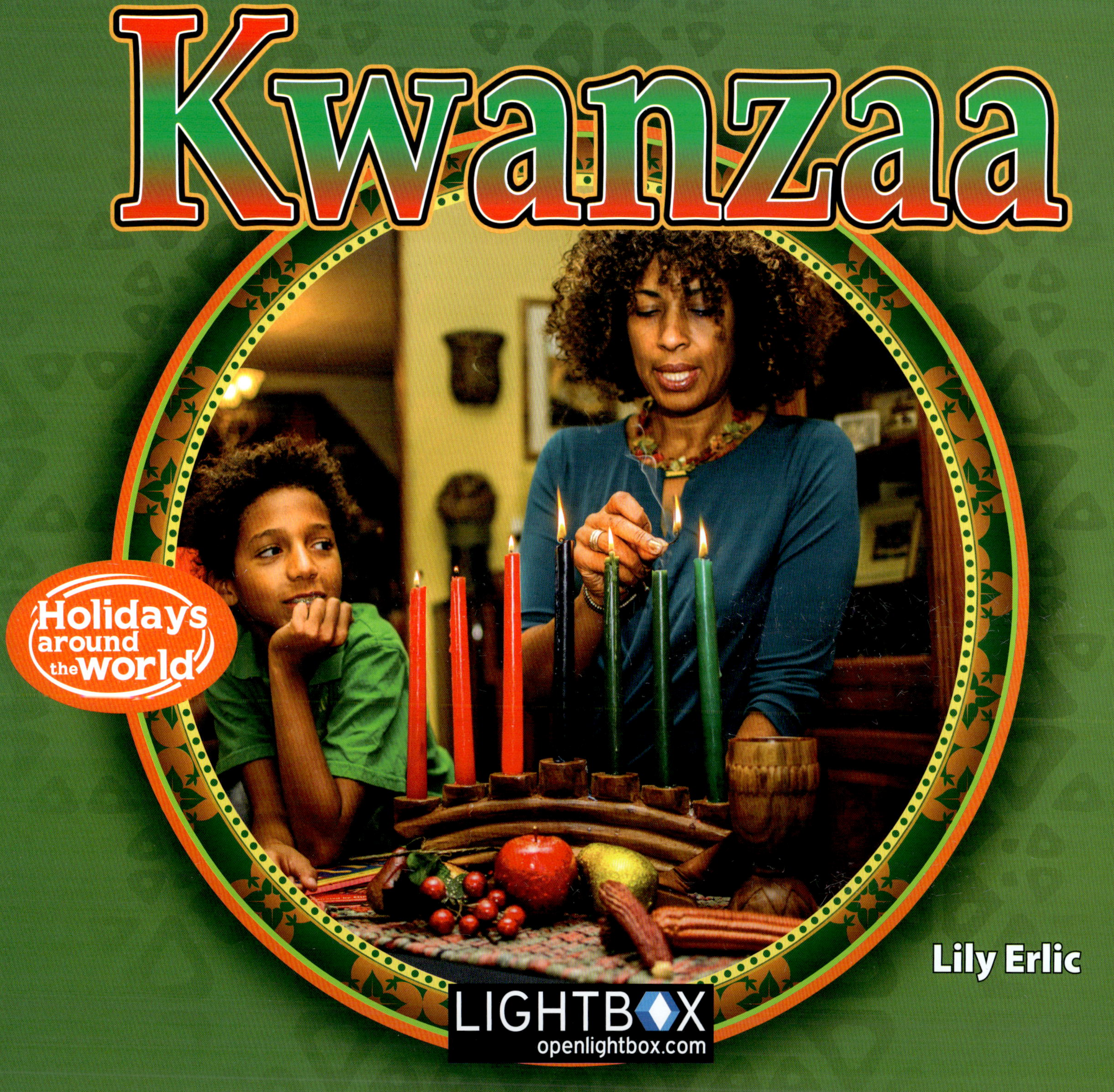

Lily Erlic

LIGHTBOX
openlightbox.com

Go to
www.openlightbox.com
and enter this book's unique code.

ACCESS CODE

LBXD8972

Lightbox is an all-inclusive digital solution for the teaching and learning of curriculum topics in an original, groundbreaking way. Lightbox is based on National Curriculum Standards.

OPTIMIZED FOR

- ✓ **TABLETS**
- ✓ **WHITEBOARDS**
- ✓ **COMPUTERS**
- ✓ **AND MUCH MORE!**

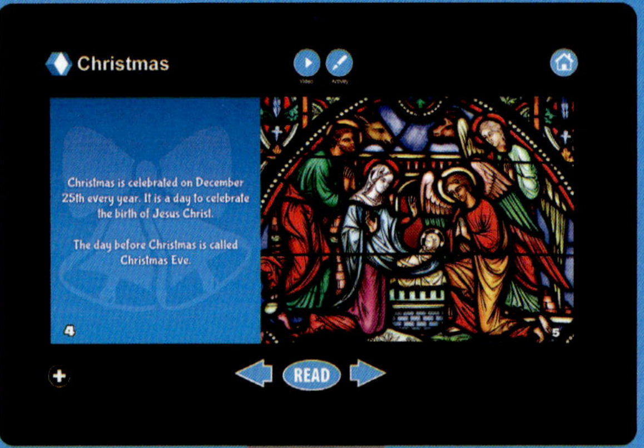

STANDARD FEATURES OF LIGHTBOX

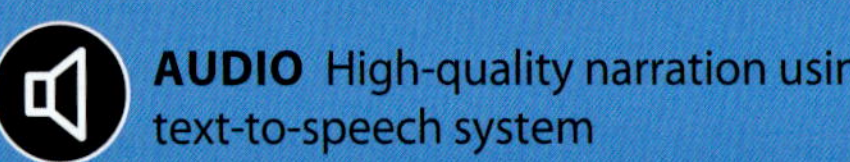
AUDIO High-quality narration using text-to-speech system

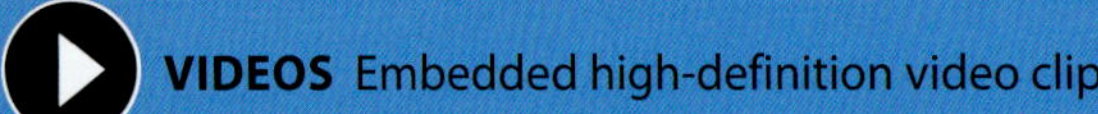
VIDEOS Embedded high-definition video clips

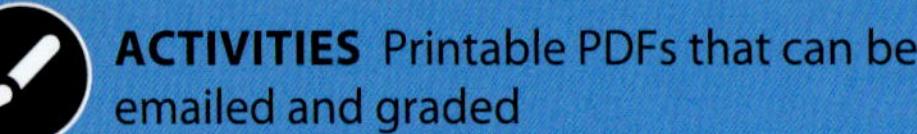
ACTIVITIES Printable PDFs that can be emailed and graded

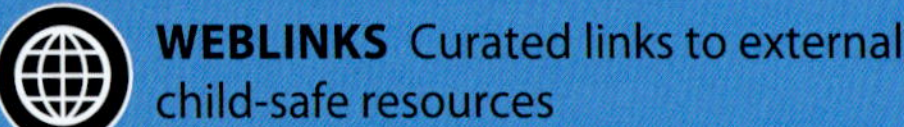
WEBLINKS Curated links to external, child-safe resources

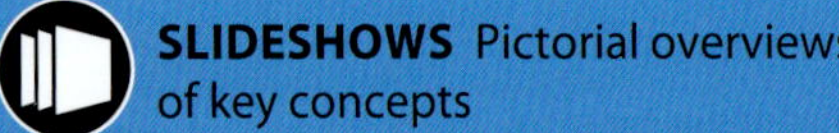
SLIDESHOWS Pictorial overviews of key concepts

INTERACTIVE MAPS Interactive maps and aerial satellite imagery

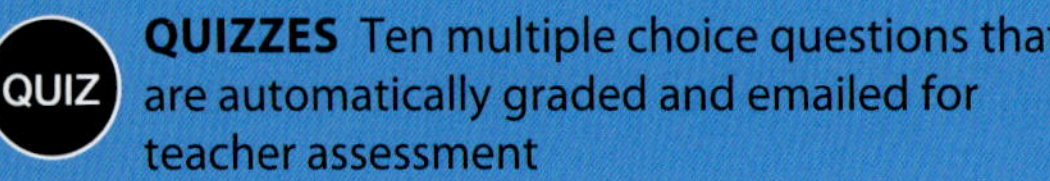
QUIZZES Ten multiple choice questions that are automatically graded and emailed for teacher assessment

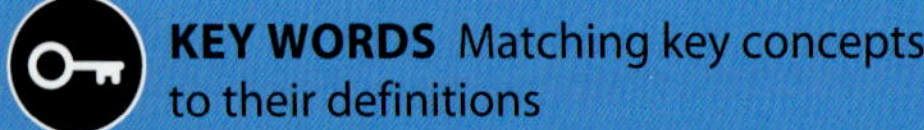
KEY WORDS Matching key concepts to their definitions

VIDEOS

WEBLINKS

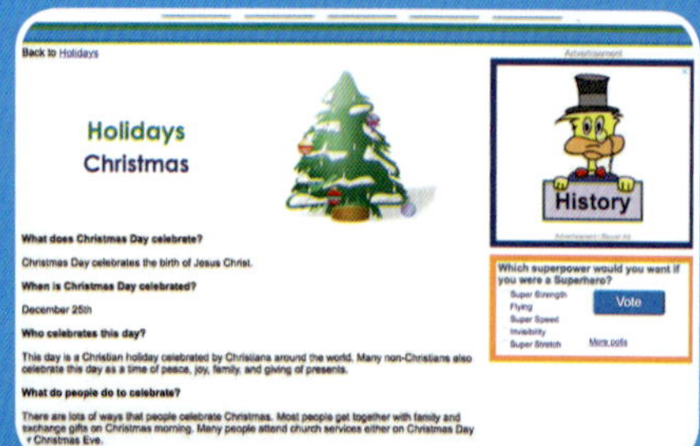

SLIDESHOWS

QUIZZES

CONTENTS

Kwanzaa is celebrated from December 26 to January 1 every year.

The holiday lasts for seven days. Each day is about one of the seven principles of Kwanzaa.

LI'L RABBIT'S KWANZAA

Kwanzaa became a holiday in **1966**.

Kwanzaa is celebrated by African Americans. It is a holiday about the importance of family.

People who live in the Caribbean celebrate, too.

Dr. Maulana Karenga is the creator of Kwanzaa. He helped African Americans remember their African culture.

TION NET
ATIONAL ACTION

Families celebrate Kwanzaa at home, community centers, and other places.

People gather in groups with their family or friends.

One of the largest Kwanzaa celebrations is at the American Museum of Natural History in New York City.

People come together to do special activities during Kwanzaa. They tell stories and read poetry.

Families celebrate Kwanzaa with foods that are easy to share, such as stews.

People bake desserts with fruits.

Seven candles represent the seven principles of Kwanzaa.

The candles are placed in a holder called a *kinara*. There are three red candles, three green candles, and one black candle.

During Kwanzaa, people help each other. Some people like to volunteer or give to charity.

Music is played to celebrate Kwanzaa. People sing African songs. They beat drums and dance, too.

KWANZAA FACTS

These pages provide more detail about the interesting facts found in the book. They are intended to be used by adults as a learning support to help young readers round out their knowledge of each holiday featured in the *Holidays around the World* series.

Pages 4–5

Kwanzaa is celebrated from December 26 to January 1 every year. The word Kwanzaa comes from a Swahili phrase, *matunda ya kwanza*. This means "first fruits." Swahili is a commonly spoken language in some parts of Africa.

Pages 6–7

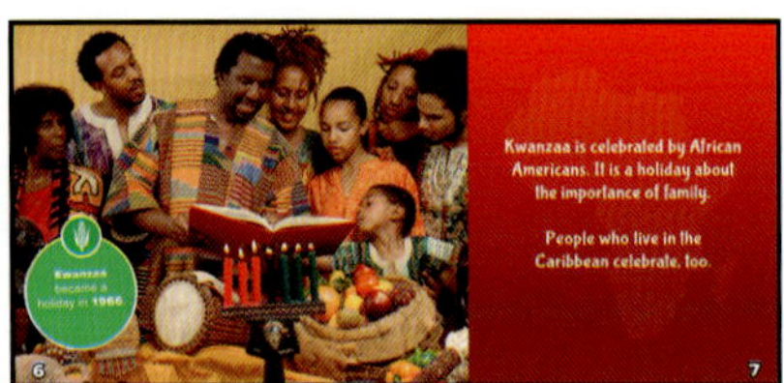

Kwanzaa is celebrated by African Americans. Today, Kwanzaa is celebrated with the same traditions that it has had since it began in 1966. The traditions of Kwanzaa come from the culture in Africa. Kwanzaa is based on harvest celebrations that have been taking place in Africa for thousands of years. Kwanzaa customs and values stem from many African customs, such as having a family feast and giving small gifts.

Pages 8–9

Dr. Maulana Karenga is the creator of Kwanzaa. He created seven important principles that are celebrated on each of the seven days. Dr. Karenga created the holiday so that African American families can enjoy family time. He also wanted African American families to remember their homeland, Africa. On the first day of Kwanzaa, unity (*umoja*) of family and community is celebrated.

Pages 10–11

Families celebrate Kwanzaa at home, community centers, and other places. Many people celebrate Kwanzaa in large groups. A candle is lit on every day of Kwanzaa. Each candle represents an important principle that is special to African Americans. The principles are unity, self-determination, collective responsibility, cooperative economics, purpose, creativity, and faith.

Pages 12–13

People come together to do special activities during Kwanzaa. This includes dressing up in African clothing. They also light the candles. Families and friends gather to show their respect to the culture of their African ancestors. Many people in Europe and Africa celebrate Kwanzaa, too.

Pages 14–15

Families celebrate Kwanzaa with foods that are easy to share, such as stews. Many families come together to eat a meal on each day of Kwanzaa. There are many dishes with African and African American roots, such as Ghanaian groundnut stew or catfish. Most of the food is homemade. Some dishes are sweet, such as candied yams. On the last day of Kwanzaa, families gather to eat a large feast.

Pages 16–17

Seven candles represent the seven principles of Kwanzaa. The lighting of a candle on each day of Kwanzaa began in 1966. Dr. Karenga was the first person to think of lighting the candle. He said it was important to think of good things such as family, friends, and community when lighting the candle. He also wanted people to remember the first harvests in Africa as a reminder to be thankful.

Pages 18–19

During Kwanzaa, people help each other. On the third day of Kwanzaa, people celebrate *ujima*. Ujima is an African word that means working together and helping each other in the community. People solve their problems together.

Pages 20–21

Music is played to celebrate Kwanzaa. African American and traditional African music is played during this holiday. Drums are played, too. Some people sing at home, concerts, or churches. Many people like to watch traditional African dances.

KEY WORDS

Research has shown that as much as 65 percent of all written material published in English is made up of 300 words. These 300 words cannot be taught using pictures or learned by sounding them out. They must be recognized by sight. This book contains 53 common sight words to help young readers improve their reading fluency and comprehension. This book also teaches young readers several important content words, such as proper nouns. These words are paired with pictures to aid in learning and improve understanding.

Page	Sight Words First Appearance
4	about, days, each, every, for, from, is, lasts, of, one, the, to, year
6	a, in
7	Americans, by, family, it, live, people, too, who
8	he, their
11	and, at, city, groups, home, new, or, other, places, with
12	come, do, read, tell, they, together
15	are, as, foods, such, that
16	there, three
19	give, help, like, some
20	songs

Page	Content Words First Appearance
4	December, holiday, January, Kwanzaa, principles
7	African Americans, Caribbean, importance
8	creator, culture, Dr. Maulana Karenga
11	American Museum of Natural History, celebrations, community centers, friends, New York City
12	activities, poetry, stories
15	desserts, fruits, stews
16	black, candles, green, holder, kinara, red
19	charity
20	drums, music

Published by Smartbook Media Inc.
350 5th Avenue, 59th Floor New York, NY 10118
Website: www.openlightbox.com

Library of Congress Cataloging-in-Publication Data

Names: Erlic, Lily, author.
Title: Kwanzaa / Lily Erlic.
Description: New York : Smartbook Media Inc., 2021. | Series: Holidays around the world | Audience: Ages 5-7 | Audience: Grades K-1 |
Identifiers: LCCN 2020004807 (print) | LCCN 2020004808 (ebook) | ISBN 9781510553255 (library binding) | ISBN 9781510553262 | ISBN 9781510553279
Subjects: LCSH: Kwanzaa--Juvenile literature. | African Americans--Social life and customs--Juvenile literature.
Classification: LCC GT4403 .E75 2021 (print) | LCC GT4403 (ebook) | DDC 394.2612--dc23
LC record available at https://lccn.loc.gov/2020004807
LC ebook record available at https://lccn.loc.gov/2020004808

032020
110819

Printed in Guangzhou, China
1 2 3 4 5 6 7 8 9 0 24 23 22 21 20

Project Coordinator: Priyanka Das
Art Director: Terry Paulhus

The publisher acknowledges Alamy, Dreamstime, Getty Images, iStock, and Newscom as its primary image suppliers for this title.